Native Americans

Southwest Indians

Mir Tamim Ansary

Heinemann Library
Chicago, Illinois

Customer Service: 888-454-2279

Designed by Depke Design

Printed in Hong Kong

04 03 02 01
10 9 8 7 6 5 4 3

Library of Congress Cataloging-in-Publication Data
Ansary, Mir Tamim
        Southwest Indians / Mir Tamim Ansary.
          p. cm. – (Native Americans)
        Includes bibliographical references and index.
        Summary: Introduces the history, dwellings, artwork, religious
beliefs, clothing, food, and other elements of life of the Native
American tribes of the Southwest.
        ISBN 1-57572-923-7
        1. Indians of North America—Southwest, New Juvenile literature.
        [1. Indians of North America—Southwest, New.] I. Title.
        II. Series: Ansary, Mir Tamim. Native Americans.
        E78.S7A67 1999
        979'.00497—dc21   99-13518
                                                              CIP

Acknowledgments
The publishers would like to thank the following for permission to reproduce photographs:
Cover: Phil Degginger/Dr. E.R. Degginger
Photo Researchers, Inc./Winston H. Sutter, pp. 4; Dr. E.R. Degginger, pp. 6, 11, 29; Phil
Degginger/Dr. E.R. Degginger, pp. 8, 9, 15; The Granger Collection, pp. 10, 22, 24, 26, 30 top;
Lawrence Migdale, pp. 12, 19; North Wind Pictures, pp. 13, 16, 25; Photo Researchers, Inc./Jeff
Greenberg, p. 14; Photo Researchers, Inc./Russell D. Curtis, p. 17; Photo Researchers, Inc./Chris
Marona, p. 18; Tristan Boyer, p. 20; Photo Researchers, Inc./Emil Muench, p. 21; Photo
Researchers, Inc./Paolo Koch, p. 27; Joel Gordon, p. 28; Corbis-Bettmann, p. 30 bottom.

Every effort has been made to contact copyright holders of any material reproduced in this
book. Any omissions will be rectified in subsequent printings if notice is given to the publisher.

Our special thanks to Lana Grant, Native American MLS, for her help
in the preparation of this book.

Note to the Reader Some words are shown in bold, **like this.** You can find
out what they mean by looking in the glossary.

Contents

The Southwest

A flat, stony desert stretches along the U.S. and Mexico border. It goes from southern Texas across New Mexico and Arizona. Flat-topped hills called *mesas* rise from these plains. In the north, these plains turn into cliffs, canyons, and mountains. This whole area is called the Southwest.

The Southwest is hot and very dry. Big rivers flow out of the mountains, but there is very little rainfall. Cactus grows wild in the south. Tough shrubs and scattered pine trees cover the slopes in the north. But in many parts of this area, the mountains are just bare, red rock.

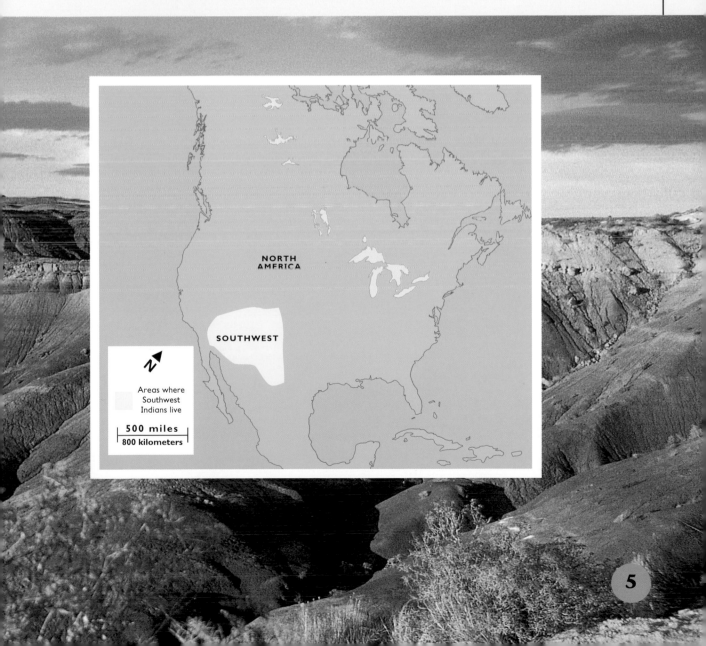

NORTH AMERICA

SOUTHWEST

Areas where Southwest Indians live

500 miles
800 kilometers

Farmers and Raiders

People first came to the Southwest during the **ice age,** more than ten thousand years ago. They were hunters chasing big animals. They also gathered wild plants. Later, they learned to grow corn and became farmers. One group, called the Anasazi, built towns high in cliffs. Their **descendants** are the Hopi and Zuni, or Pueblo Indians, of today.

The Ansazi built their villages in cliffs.

Around the year 1500, some new tribes came into this region. These people were the Navajo and Apache. They were **raiders.** They had been wandering south from Canada for some time. They attacked Pueblo Indian villages. The farmers fought back. Over time, however, the raiders learned much from the farmers.

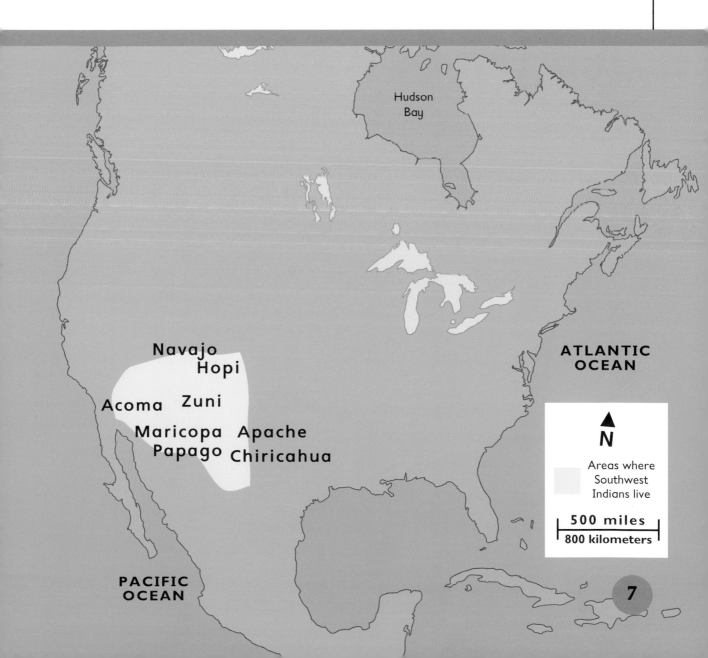

Hudson Bay

Navajo
Hopi

Acoma   Zuni

Maricopa   Apache
Papago   Chiricahua

ATLANTIC OCEAN

N

Areas where Southwest Indians live

500 miles
800 kilometers

PACIFIC OCEAN

Native American Foods

The farmers of the Southwest grew beans, squash, and other vegetables. But their main **crop** was corn. They developed a new type of corn. It had kernels of many colors, such as blue and red. This type of corn grew well in the dry Southwest because it didn't need much water.

Today, "Indian" corn is sometimes used as decoration because it is colorful.

The Navajo learned sheep herding from the Pueblo Indians.

Once the **raiders** settled in the Southwest, they learned to farm. They tended small, widely scattered gardens. The Navajo also started herding sheep for meat and wool. Sheep could live on the short, tough grass found here. But families had to move to new **pastures** from season to season.

Pueblos and Hogans

Tribes such as the Hopi and Zuni were called Pueblo Indians because they lived in pueblos. Pueblos were like big apartment buildings. Each one was a town with many one-room houses joined together. Each pueblo ruled itself and was separate from other pueblos. The group of people in a pueblo was also called a pueblo.

The word pueblo comes from a Spanish word meaning "town."

For religious reasons, the door of a hogan always faces east.

The Navajo and Apache did not crowd together. The Navajo, for example, built hogans. These round houses stood alone. Hogans in a Navajo area were spread far apart. Early hogans were made of poles, **brush,** and mud. If a family decided to move, they could quickly build a new hogan.

Clothing Over Time

Since the Southwest is hot, the Pueblo wore light cotton clothing. Long ago, the Pueblo mostly wore **kilts** and wraps. Later, they began wearing European-style dresses and pants. Unmarried Pueblo girls wore their hair in "squash blossoms." These were big buns, one above each ear.

Pueblo Indians made ornaments out of shells and blue stones called turquoise.

These Mescalero Apaches are wearing garments of cloth as well as fur. The man on the left is wearing a Navajo blanket.

The ancient Navajo and Apache wore clothes made of softened deer leather, also called buckskin. They decorated the buckskin with beads. Later, they too began wearing cloth garments. The poncho, for example, was a blanket that could be worn like a shirt. It had a hole in the middle for the person's head to fit through.

Arts of the Southwest

The Pueblo Indians were great potters. Pueblo potters were usually women. They stacked up coils of clay by hand. Each coil was a bit bigger or smaller than the one before. In this way, the pot took a certain shape. Today, Pueblo artists are again making pots in this way.

Southwest Indians have been making pottery for at least 4,000 years.

14

Most Navajo weavers now make blankets to sell, not to use themselves.

The Navajo learned to weave from the Pueblo people. They became the finest weavers in the Southwest. The Navajo wove beautiful woolen rugs and blankets on simple wooden frames. Long ago, the Navajo saw weaving as a job for men. But today, Navajo women are weavers, too.

Daily Life in a Pueblo

In a pueblo, all wealth was shared. But life was carefully planned. Each person and group had certain jobs set by custom. Women, for example, ground corn. They used two stone tools called the *mano* and *metate*. Since corn was very important in Pueblo life, this work was highly honored.

These Pueblo women are using manos to grind corn on stone metates.

Some Pueblo ceremonies last as long as nine days.

Men were in charge of religious work. They spent
as much as half their time performing **ceremonies.**
The ceremonies were meant to keep the whole
group in **harmony** with nature. Such harmony, they
believed, brought, health, rain, and other good luck.
Other Native Americans of the Southwest shared
such beliefs.

Kachinas and Kivas

Most Pueblo people believe in helpful **spirits** called *kachinas.* In certain **ceremonies,** men wear masks that stand for kachinas. In these masks, they believe, they become kachinas. Hopi children play with kachina dolls. From these beautiful toys, they learn the religious beliefs of their people.

Among the ancient Hopi, both boys and girls played with kachina dolls.

Kachina masks and other sacred objects were stored in the kiva.

Every pueblo has an underground religious room called a kiva. In the middle of this room is a deep pit. Kivas were found even in the ancient cities of the Anasazi. The kiva is a **sacred** place. Outsiders are usually not allowed inside. In ancient times, only men could enter the kiva.

Myths and Healing Chants

Many Southwest Indians believe that time is divided into **stages**. Hopi myths, for example, say there are four such stages. In the first three stages, people lived underground. Then they climbed out through a cave called *Sipapu*. The pit in a kiva stands for this cave.

sipapu.

The pit in a kiva stood for a sacred cave known as sipapu.

There are more than 800 forms of sand paintings.
Each goes with a different chant.

The Navajo express myths and religious ideas in sand paintings. These are made of colored sand by religious experts called medicine men. A sand painting is usually part of a healing **ceremony.** It goes with certain chants and dances. Soon after the ceremony, the medicine man erases the painting.

Europeans Arrive

Francisco Coronado was the first European to reach the Southwest. He came here in 1540. This Spanish explorer was looking for cities of gold. He found only pueblos of clay. Even so, Spanish armies followed in his footsteps. They conquered the Pueblo people and took over the Southwest.

Coronado destroyed many Indian towns in his search for gold.

The Pueblo Indians stayed away from the Spanish as best they could. Each pueblo chose one man to talk to the Spanish leaders when needed. All the others stayed near their pueblos. In 1848, the Southwest became part of the United States. But the pueblos remained very private.

The Wars

The Apaches and Navajo tried to fight the white settlers. These wars started in the 1860s. Great chiefs such as Cochise and Mangas Colorado led the Apache. The last great Apache warrior was Geronimo. He fought the U.S. Army until 1886. The Apache quit fighting when Geronimo was sent to prison in Florida.

Geronimo died in 1909, after living 23 years as a prisoner.

IN COMMEMORATION OF THE NAVAJOS
WHO LIVED HERE IN EXILE, 1863-1868.
THE CENTENNIAL RE-ENACTMENT OF THE
SIGNING OF THE TREATY OF PEACE (1 JUNE 1868)
TOOK PLACE ON THIS SPOT.
ERECTED BY THE NAVAJO TRIBE AND THE
PLATEAU SCIENCES SOCIETY, WINDOW ROCK,
ARIZONA, FEBRUARY 1971.

"The Long Walk" took about nineteen days to complete.

A soldier named Kit Carson defeated the Navajo. He made them leave their home in Arizona. He marched them 300 miles (483 kilometers) to Basque Redondo, New Mexico. The Navajo call that journey "The Long Walk." In New Mexico, the Navajo had no farms or flocks of sheep. After four hard years, they got a **reservation** back in their homeland in Arizona.

Old and New

In the early 1900s, the U.S. government tried to make the Native Americans be like white Americans. Children were sent to boarding schools and taught to speak English. They were made to dress and act like white Americans. But most Southwest Indians held onto their own ways.

At the Carlisle Indian School in Pennsylvania, Indian children were taught white customs.

Sheep herding remains important on the Navajo reservation.

The Navajo **reservation** is now the largest in the country. The land has oil, **uranium,** silver, and other riches. Many of the people, however, are still poor. The Navajo tribe is building modern businesses. It is trying to keep the Navajo way of life going, too. Doing both is not easy.

The Southwest Today

Today, the Southwest Indians are known throughout the world for their arts and crafts. Navajo silver work is sold in faraway cities like New York. Zuni pots are shown in art **galleries** across the country. **Tourists** from many countries come to the Southwest to buy these works of art.

The Navajo learned silversmithing from the Mexicans in the 19th century.

People have been living in Taos Pueblo for almost 1,000 years.

But there is a world tourists rarely see. It lies beyond the trading posts. It lies behind the walls of pueblos like Acoma and Taos. There, in America's oldest cities, an ancient way of life goes on. It is the peaceful way born among the Anasazi a long time ago.

Famous Southwest Indians

Cochise (Apache: 1815–1874) Cochise was a great Chiricahua Apache chief. In 1862, the U.S. Army killed some of his people, and Cochise went to war. He did not quit fighting until 1872. That year, a **reservation** was set aside for Apaches in Arizona. Cochise lived there peacefully until his death.

Peter McDonald (Navajo: 1925–) McDonald was the leader of the Navajo Tribal Council from 1971 to 1981. He was the only man elected to the job three times. McDonald worked for Navajo control of the Navajo reservation. He also helped the tribe build modern businesses.

Maria Martinez (San Ildefonso Pueblo: 1887–1980) Martinez brought a lost craft back to life. She learned how the ancient Pueblos had made pots and started to make new pots in those forgotten ways. Other Pueblo learned her techniques. Today, pottery is an important Pueblo business.

Glossary

brush thick growth of weeds and shrubs mixed with broken branches

ceremony set of acts that has religious meaning

crop farm product, usually a plant grown for food

descendant person's child, grandchild, and so on

gallery place where art is shown and sometimes sold

harmony going well together

ice age time in history when much of the earth was covered with ice

kilt knee-length skirt worn by men or women

mineral rock or soil that has metal or other useful parts

pasture open grassland where animals eat

raider person who attacks others to take their goods

reservation land set aside for Native Americans

sacred that which is treated with great respect for religious reasons

spirit being that has life but cannot be seen

stage part that comes one after another or in layers.

tourist person who visits a place to see the sights

uranium rocklike material used to make atom bombs

More Books to Read

Lund, Bill. *The Apache Indians.* Danbury, Conn.: Children's Press, 1997.

Petersen, David. *The Anasazi.* Danbury, Conn.: Children's Press, 1991.

Ross, Pamela. *The Pueblo Indians.* Mankato, Minn.: Capstone Press, 1999.

Sneve, Virginia D. *The Navajos: A First Americans Book.* New York: Holiday House, 1993.

Index